New Wine into Old Wineskins

New Wine into Old Wineskins

JONATHAN FEATHERS

RESOURCE *Publications* • Eugene, Oregon

NEW WINE INTO OLD WINESKINS

Resource Publications
An Imprint of Wipf and Stock Publishers
199 W. 8th Ave., Suite 3
Eugene, OR 97401

www.wipfandstock.com

ISBN 13: 978-1-4982-2170-2

Manufactured in the U.S.A.

To Melanie, Dorothy, and all who have encouraged
me in ministry.

Commit to the Lord whatever you do, and your plans will succeed.

PROVERBS 16:3 NIV

CONTENTS

Introduction

Challenge

The Issue

IN THE BOOK, *THE Ascent of a Leader*, the authors write, "the ability to initiate and sustain positive cultural changes may prove to be the single greatest need of twenty-first century organizations."[1] Change is needed in order to survive in the world. Whether we like it or not, change is here to stay. We must learn from change, become familiar with change, and utilize change.

Change exists on personal, organizational, and global levels. For instance, personal changes occur when we face a job-loss or move from one location to another. Organizational change takes place when a new leader emerges. Global change happens constantly and often unexpectedly in the form of environmental and natural disasters. Change exists all around us all the time.

It is natural then that churches deal with change as well. Independent Bible-believing churches, such as those within the Restoration Movement (referred to as independent Christian Churches/Churches of Christ), commonly struggle with change. This is true for Restoration Movement churches ranging from two members to 20,000 members. The struggle lies partially in the fact that the independent churches do not function underneath a denominational hierarchy. Mark Taylor writes, "Christian churches and churches of Christ form a thriving independent fellowship.

1. Thrall et al, *The Ascent of a Leader*, 26.

We have no hierarchy, no regional offices, no bishop or district minister telling us what to do or who our next minister will be."[2] There are many lay leaders who have little formal theological education or ministry experience, and when it comes to change they are not always prepared for the process.

I served a church that faced change. I began serving as the senior minister at this particular church in 2009. The previous senior minister retired after serving this church for over forty years. This church began in 1955 when a group of Christians met in a home. The group of believers discussed the possibility of planting a new congregation on the west side of town. The group met at a school until property was purchased and a building constructed. In 1957 the building was dedicated for use. From 1955 to 2009, only three senior ministers served this church. After a more than forty year tenure of the previous senior minister, just the presence of a new senior minister was a major change for the church. Many people had built strong relationships with the previous senior minister, and the change was grieved much like a death. Over the past forty years, the average Sunday attendance increased to over 300 and then declined to about 150. As the new senior minister, I thought it would be vital for the impact of my ministry to address the change process.

Change Process Defined

For the purpose of this book, the change process will be defined as: A change process involves focusing on the mission, clarifying the values, aligning the strategy, and casting a vision for this church.

The Proposal

This book addresses the question, how can a church implement a change process? However, there are several additional questions which must also be addressed before a solution is reached.

2. Taylor, "Help for the Time You Hire a New Minister," 3.

- Why change?
- How have some organizations encountered the change process?
- What methods are currently available to implement the change process?
- What would a change process include?
- How can a church implement a change process?

By answering each of these additional questions, a better understanding will be gained of what a change process is, what a change process does, why a change process is important, and how a change process can be implemented for a church. The more the church understands the change process the better it can implement changes.

The Project

This book, this case study, integrates many of the concepts and methods of Jim Collins' *Built to Last* and John Kotter's *Leading Change* with an established church. By utilizing these resources, a series of workshops were developed that aimed to:

- focus on the mission of a church
- clarify the values of a church
- align the strategy of a church
- cast a vision of a church

By developing and facilitating a series of workshops, I initiated a change process.

Chapter one deals with the theological framework by examining characters and biblical passages that address the biblical mission of the church. Chapter two reviews the concepts and methods of Jim Collins' book *Built to Last* and John Kotter's book *Leading Change* in order to implement the change process at the church where I served. Chapter three describes several workshops that I developed using the concepts and methods of *Built to Last* and

Leading Change. The goal of these workshops was to facilitate the change process for this church by focusing on the mission, clarifying the values, aligning the strategy, and casting a vision. Chapter four assesses the workshops and introduces the change process for a church. The Appendices include handouts for the workshops and my commentary on the handouts

In the article, "The Leader's New Work: Building Learning Organizations," Peter M. Senge writes, "the first task of organization design concerns designing the governing ideas of purpose, vision, and core values."[3] As this church embarked on a journey with a new senior minister, I thought it would be appropriate to set the course. This church, as with any organization, should at least understand its mission; or as Jim Collins suggests, understand its core ideology and envisioned future.[4] The change process sought to define and articulate the core ideology and envisioned future, using John Kotter's eight-stage process of creating major change. As the new senior minister, I possessed a unique opportunity to reflect and evaluate the mission and culture of this church and to cast a vision for the future this church.

3. Senge, "The Leader's New Work: Building Learning Organizations," 7–23.

4. Collins, *Built to Last*, 220.

I

Wine and Wineskins

one

Command

THE TOPIC OF DEVELOPING a mission statement is rather broad and extensive. Much has been written about how to develop a mission statement for businesses—whether profit or non-profit—and churches. Much can be learned about why it is important to clearly articulate and understand such a statement. Before proceeding, it is necessary to understand how a church can work towards fulfilling the biblical mission in light of a business mission statement. This chapter will attempt to answer the following questions:

1. What is a mission?
2. What is a business's mission?
3. What is a church's mission?
4. How can a church work towards fulfilling the biblical mission?

What Is A Mission?

What is a mission? To a business, a mission explains its reason for existence. To a church, the mission determines its primary focus. Both businesses and churches strive to fulfill what they set out to do. If a mission is not clearly stated then a business, or a church, may lose focus and eventually decline or cease to exist. Jim Collins and Jerry Porras write, "They understand that contentment leads to complacency, which inevitably leads to decline."[1] In both, business and churches, the leadership must understand and communicate its mission. In their book, *Spiritual Leadership*, Henry and Richard Blackaby write about the need for effective leaders in both businesses and churches. In regard to business leaders, they write, "Today's leaders must mold productive, cohesive teams out of the most diverse workforce in history. Leaders are expected to gain new skills continually and to adjust to dizzying daily changes in the business world."[2] In regard to church leaders, they write, "In order to survive, churches are seeking leaders who can not only overcome the voluminous challenges churches are facing, but also attract new members and resources in order to finance an increasingly expensive organization."[3] In addressing this dilemma, the Blackabys raise an interesting point, "The issue of leadership holds a deeper dimension for Christians: Is Christian leadership the same thing as secular leadership?"[4] This question poses another question for the church leader, "Do leadership principles found in secular writing and seminars apply to work done in God's kingdom?"[5] Henry and Richard offer a strong conclusion:

> Christian leaders who know God and who know how to lead in a Christian manner will be phenomenally more effective in their world than even the most skilled and qualified leaders who lead without God. Spiritual leadership is not restricted to pastors and missionaries. It is the responsibility of all Christians whom God wants to use to make a difference in their world. The challenge for today's leaders is to discern the difference between the latest leadership fads and timeless truths established by God.[6]

1. Collins and Porras, *Built to Last*, 187.
2. Blackaby and Blackaby, *Spiritual Leadership*, 7.
3. Ibid., *Spiritual Leadership*, 9.
4. Ibid., *Spiritual Leadership*, 9.
5. Ibid., *Spiritual Leadership*, 9.
6. Ibid., *Spiritual Leadership*, 14.

Leaders, whether in a business or a church, affect the mission and direction of an organization. Here are a few examples of how leadership is defined:

a. "Leadership is the process of persuasion or example by which an individual (or a leadership team) induces a group to pursue objectives held by a leader or shared by the leader and his or her followers."[7]

b. "Leadership is influence, the ability of one person to influence others."[8]

c. "A Christian leader is someone who is called by God to lead; leads with and through Christlike character; and demonstrates the functional competencies that permit effective leadership to take place."[9]

If these few suggestions illuminate what leaders do, then leaders must work at discerning and defining the mission and how that mission is executed for their business or church.

Leaders help define the mission. Warren Bennis writes, "The task of the leader is to define the mission."[10] In his book, *Advanced Strategic Planning*, Aubrey Malphurs states, "The ministry's mission is important because it affects the church in a number of essential ways."[11] Malphurs addresses the need for churches to revisit the biblical passages because "a mission for a church must be based on the Scriptures."[12] Malphurs states, "The development of an effective, biblical mission statement should be the goal of every church leader."[13] He encourages church leaders to contemplate what the mission of the church is. He goes on to challenge church leaders to consider asking the following questions:

7. Gardner, *On Leadership*, 1.

8. Sanders, *Spiritual Leadership*, 19.

9. Barna, *Leaders on Leadership*, 25.

10. Bennis, *On Becoming a Leader*, 183.

11. Malphurs, *Advanced Strategic Planning*, 120.

12. Ibid., *Advanced Strategic Planning*, 127.

13. Ibid., *Advanced Strategic Planning*, 119.

1. What is the church supposed to be doing?
2. What is this church doing?
3. Why are you not doing what you are supposed to be doing?
4. What will it take for you to change and do what you are supposed to be doing?[14]

Jim Collins and Jim Porras urge organizations to understand their core ideology.[15] They claim that, "Core ideology provides the bonding glue that holds an organization together as it grows, decentralizes, diversifies, expands globally, and attains diversity within."[16] A mission attempts to explain why an organization does what it does.

Andy Stanley and Bill Willits give an appropriate example of how this is true for the church as well:

> After welcoming people to "No Point" church, Andy reminded us that this was an issue with a lot of churches. They had lost their point, and we needed to make sure that we stayed on mission so we didn't follow suit. The signage that night made us laugh, but it also provided a subtle reminder for us to say focused on what God had called us to do.[17]

Stanley and Willits share their perspective on how churches may describe their mission as either being a skill-based church; one that, "seems to be on people becoming proficient and effective in certain skills;" or a Bible-knowledge church, one that exists to "help people to become biblically literate."[18] In order to resolve this tension, Stanley and Willits offer five questions:

1. Why is it important for an organization to have a clearly defined mission statement?
2. What is the mission of your church?
3. How would you define a disciple?

14. Malphurs, *Advanced Strategic Planning*, 128.

15. Collins and Porras, *Built to Last*, 48.

16. Ibid., *Built to Last*, 221.

17. Stanley and Willits, *Creating Community*, 52.

18. Ibid., *Creating Community*, 55.

4. What do you want the people you influence to become?
5. How has this been communicated to them?[19]

Rick Warren asks a similar question in *The Purpose Driven Church*:

> Every church is driven by something. There is a guiding force, a controlling assumption, a directing conviction behind everything that happens. It may be unspoken. It may be unknown to many. Most likely it's never been officially voted on. But it is there, influencing every aspect of the church's life. What is the driving force behind your church?[20]

Warren proposes that churches determine their purpose because "It is not merely a target that you aim for; it is your congregation's reason for being."[21] In understanding a church's purpose, or mission, Rick Rusaw and Eric Swanson present a compelling argument:

> How many times does it take to create a church tradition? Only once . . . if it is successful. The methodologies that we currently use are the answers to the tough questions a previous generation (or two . . . or three) asked. The toughest programs to kill are those that are working. Remember that we organize around purpose, not around program or tactic. Every program that is effective today, no matter how good it is, has a life span. It eventually will lose momentum. We've got to be so in tune with God's purpose that our purpose isn't interrupted when a program runs out of steam.[22]

One can conclude that a major function of a leader is to define the mission of the business or church. A primary function of a leader is to regularly and consistently remind the business or church of its mission. If a leader is not effectively communicating

19. Stanley and Willits, *Creating Community*, 59.
20. Warren, *The Purpose Driven Church*, 77.
21. Ibid., *The Purpose Driven Church*, 109.
22. Rusaw & Swanson, *The Externally Focused Church*, 203.

or evaluating its mission then the business or church can get off course and lose sight of what it was originally setting out to accomplish. In his book, *When God Builds a Church*, Bob Russell writes, "It's easy for any enterprise to get sidetracked from its main thrust."[23] Russell gives a humorous example, "I ate at a restaurant recently called The Pancake Factory. You know what their luncheon special was that day? Grilled chicken sandwich with spicy Mexican sauce. I was convinced that they had lost their focus."[24] Russell goes on to say, "The church, like that restaurant, can easily get sidetracked and forget its primary mission."[25] Aubrey Malphurs strongly urges churches to regularly ask three critical questions:

1. What are we supposed to be doing?

2. Are we doing it?

3. If not, why not?[26]

These three questions serve as a catalyst in reminding a church of its original mission. These same questions could be applied to a business as well. Either way, a leader must be able to discover and articulate the mission of the organization or church. At this point it is worthwhile to examine the mission of a business.

WHAT IS A BUSINESS' MISSION?

A business' mission describes its objective, or what it hopes to achieve in order to determine its success. Jim Collins and Jerry Porras use a different terminology. Instead of using the term mission, they use the term "core purpose."[27] They write that the core purpose "is the organization's fundamental reason for being."[28] Collins and Porras also say this about a core purpose: "whereas

23. Russell, *When God Builds a Church*, 251.

24. Ibid., *When God Builds a Church*, 251.

25. Ibid., *When God Builds a Church*, 251.

26. Malphurs, *Advanced Strategic Planning*, 168.

27. Collins and Porras, *Built to Last*, 224.

28. Ibid., *Built to Last*, 224.

you might achieve a goal or complete a strategy, you cannot fulfill a purpose; it is like a guiding star on the horizon—forever pursued, but never reached. Yet while purpose itself does not change, it does inspire change."[29] The business' mission instills a level of intrinsic motivation. Collins and Porras give some examples of a core purpose for business, or in the case of this book—a mission:

> 3M:To solve unsolved problems innovatively
>
> Cargill:To improve the standard of living around the world
>
> Hewlett-Packard:To make technical contributions for the advancement and welfare of humanity
>
> Lost Arrow Corporation:To be a role model and tool for social change
>
> Mary Kay:To give unlimited opportunity to women
>
> Merck: To preserve and improve human life
>
> Walt Disney:To make people happy[30]

For many businesses, their formal written mission statement, or core purpose, can become cluttered and covered by all that the business is trying to do. In the *Harvard Business Review,* Eric Hellweg writes about such an occurrence, "Most companies, regardless of their sectors, have a mission statement. And most are awash in jargon and marble-mouthed pronouncements. Worse still, these gobbled-gook statements are often forgotten by misremembered, or flatly ignored by frontline employees."[31] It is important for a business to create a simple, yet unforgettable, mission; one that is easy for employees to remember and see how results are being achieved.

In his book, *Developing the Leaders Around You,* John Maxwell presents a compelling argument regarding the development of leaders. If a leader helps define the mission of an organization, or church, then the leader must be developing him or her and

29. Ibid., *Built to Last*, 224–225.
30. Ibid., *Built to Last*, 225.
31. Hellweg, "The Eight-Word Mission Statement".

others. Maxwell states, "Everything rises and falls on leadership."[32] As Maxwell addresses the concern of leadership, he also claims, "A company must organize around what it is trying to accomplish, not around what is being done."[33] Maxwell prepares a strong case of the need for strong leaders within an organization, or church, if it is going to fulfill its stated mission. In chapter five of *Developing the Leaders Around You*, Maxwell poses a series of questions about the organization.[34] One of the questions is

> What is the statement of purpose for the organization? The development of leaders in an organization must begin with a review of the organization's purpose. (Presumably, the purpose of your organization is already in writing. If not, write it down. Or ask someone in authority to provide you with a statement of purpose.) Don't even consider performing equipping or training that does not contribute to the fulfillment of the organization's purpose.[35]

This goes to show how leaders can affect the mission of an organization or church. If leaders are left undeveloped, then they can head off course.

Many business people have been influenced by the Bible. Notice what the following people had to say about the influence of the Bible:

> Robert E. Lee—"In all my perplexities and distresses, the Bible has never failed to give me light and strength."

> Theodore Roosevelt—"A thorough understanding of the Bible is better than a college education."

> Abraham Lincoln—"I believe the Bible is the best gift God has ever given to man."

32. Maxwell, *Developing the Leaders Around You*, 6.
33. Ibid., *Developing the Leaders Around You*, 12.
34. Ibid., *Developing the Leaders Around You*, 85.
35. Ibid., *Developing the Leaders Around You*, 85–86.

George Washington—"It is impossible to rightly govern the world without God and the Bible."[36]

In addition to these men, many business leaders such as S. Truett Cathy, David Novak, Zig Ziglar, John Maxwell and Jim Collins, refer to the influence of the Bible on their lives and businesses.[37] An article, "Christian CEO's on Leadership" from Smart Ministry, records various responses to what they "have learned about leadership and how their faith shapes their daily work and decision making."[38] Here are some of those responses:

> David Everitt—People are empowered to perform their part in accomplishing a common objective by a leader who serves and supports those he or she seeks to lead.

> John Beckett—George Mueller said, "Stick to your original vision." Each one of us is called by God to a particular sphere of activity.

> Jeff Thiemann—Study the Bible for examples of great leadership.

> David Everitt—Determine whether the primary mission of what you're responsible for is providing leadership for an organization or for people—leadership of both is necessary with any endeavor, but your leadership strategies will differ depending on which is the driving force. Determine why you do what you do in your organization in light of your Christian calling, and make sure your organization has a soul.

> Elisa Morgan—Ministry and management are linked. Neither is more vital than the other; both are intrinsic leadership responsibilities.

> John Beckett—I believe each of us can learn from Jesus' impeccable leadership example.

---

36. Harper, *Leading from the Lion's Den*, 3.
37. Harper, *Leading from the Lion's Den*, 3.
38. "Christian CEO's on Leadership," 1.

Many of these responses refer to how the Bible and Christian faith influence an individual or organizational mission. Therefore, it is important that we examine the church's mission.

WHAT IS A CHURCH'S MISSION?

In order to answer this question it is necessary to revisit the Bible. The biblical mandate and the words of Jesus function as a cornerstone in identifying the core ideology of the church. Unfortunately, there seem to be numerous churches, with differing denominational backgrounds, that wrestle with clearly articulating a church's mission. Thus, it is vital for a church to answer this clearly. This chapter will review the biblical mandate and the words of Jesus regarding fulfilling a mission and identify some biblical examples of a change process.

OLD TESTAMENT

To begin with, this chapter examines some of the characters from the Old Testament and how these characters fulfill their mission. Genesis reads "The Lord had said to Abram, "Go from your country, your people and your father's household to the land I will show you.""[39] Abram's mission is to obey the Lord. The Lord instructs Abram to leave his homeland, take what he has with him, and travel to a new, distant land. Genesis twelve describes this: "He took his wife Sarai, his nephew Lot, all the possessions they had accumulated and the people they had acquired in Harran, and they set out for the land of Canaan, and they arrived there."[40] The Bible explains how Abram continues to obey the Lord. In Genesis seventeen, the Lord says to Abram, "Then I will make my covenant between me and you and will greatly increase your numbers."[41] Genesis twenty-five states, "After Abraham's death, God blessed

39. Genesis 12:1 NIV.
40. Genesis 12:5 NIV.
41. Genesis 17:2 NIV.

his son Isaac, who then lived near Beer Lahai Roi."[42] Abram (later known as Abraham) fulfills his mission from the Lord to settle in a foreign land.

Exodus speaks of the birth of Moses and his calling—his mission from the Lord. Exodus chapters three and four explain what happens to Moses. An angel of the Lord appears to Moses "in flames of fire from within a bush."[43] In the midst of the encounter and conversation that ensues, the Lord says to Moses, "So now, go. I am sending you to Pharaoh to bring my people the Israelites out of Egypt."[44] Moses' mission is to return to Egypt, confront Pharaoh, and lead the Israelites out of Egypt. Moses doubts his abilities and questions the Lord. Eventually, Pharaoh allows Moses and the Israelites to leave Egypt. According to Exodus twelve, Pharaoh says, "Up! Leave my people, you and the Israelites! Go, worship the Lord as you have requested. Take your flocks and herds, as you have said, and go. And also bless me."[45] Moses fulfills his mission from the Lord to lead the Israelites out of Egypt.

Later, Joshua succeeds Moses. The Lord speaks to Joshua and reveals to him his mission. The Lord says to Joshua, "Be strong and courageous, because you will lead these people to inherit the land I swore to their ancestors to give them."[46] Near the end of his life, Joshua recalls all that had taken place during his lifetime and reminds the Israelites, "You yourselves have seen everything the Lord your God has done to all these nations for your sake; it was the Lord your God who fought for you. Remember how I have allotted as an inheritance for your tribes all the land of the nations that remain—the nations I conquered—between the Jordan and the Mediterranean Sea in the west."[47] Joshua fulfills his mission from the Lord to lead the Israelites to the Promised Land.

42. Genesis 25:11 NIV.
43. Exodus 3:2 NIV.
44. Exodus 3:10 NIV.
45. Exodus 12:31–32 NIV.
46. Joshua 1:6 NIV.
47. Joshua 23:3–4 NIV.

Many years later, a new king is to be anointed over Israel. While in Bethlehem, Samuel anoints a young man who is "He was glowing with health and had a fine appearance and handsome features."[48] After the anointing, 1 Samuel sixteen records that "from that day on the Spirit of the Lord came powerfully upon David."[49] David becomes the new king of Israel. Over the course of his lifetime, David fulfills his mission from the Lord to be the ruler of Israel.

Soon after David's death, his son Solomon pursues the task of constructing a Temple for the Lord. In a message, Solomon states,

> You know that because of the wars waged against my father David from all sides, he could not build a temple for the Name of the Lord his God until the Lord put his enemies under his feet. But now the Lord my God has given me rest on every side, and there is no adversary or disaster. I intend, therefore, to build a temple for the Name of the Lord my God, as the Lord told my father David, when he said, 'Your son whom I will put on the throne in your place will build the temple for my Name.'[50]

It takes Solomon seven years to build the Temple.[51] Solomon fulfills his mission from the Lord to construct a Temple.

After Solomon's death, the nation of Israel is split between Solomon's sons, Rehoboam and Jeroboam. Rehoboam is the king of Judah, while Jeroboam is the king of Israel.[52] Over the course of several hundreds of years, Israel and Judah fall to the Persians and Babylonians. The people are scattered throughout the land. Some remain in their homelands, while others are forced into slavery or become citizens in their captor's kingdom. During the exiles, others are given a mission to fulfill.

While in captivity to the Persians, Mordecai discovers a plot to destroy the Jews. Mordecai reports this to Esther, a Jewish

48. 1 Samuel 16:12 NIV.
49. 1 Samuel 16:13 NIV.
50. 1 Kings 5:3–5 NIV.
51. 1 Kings 6:38 NIV.
52. 1 Kings 12–14 NIV.

woman who has been made queen. Once the conspiracy is disclosed, Mordecai responds,

> Do not think that because you are in the king's house you alone of all the Jews will escape. For if you remain silent at this time, relief and deliverance for the Jews will arise from another place, but you and your father's family will perish. And who knows but that you have come to your royal position for such a time as this?[53]

In due time, the conspiracy is made known to King Xerxes, who has the conspirators hanged. Esther fulfills her mission from the Lord to deliver the Jews.

Eventually, some of the Israelite captives are allowed to return to their homeland around Jerusalem. King Artaxerxes gives permission to Nehemiah to return to Jerusalem and rebuild it. In fifty-two days, the wall surrounding Jerusalem had been rebuilt.[54] Nehemiah fulfills his mission from the Lord to return to Jerusalem and rebuild its walls.

Each of these characters possess a specific mission which they are to fulfill. Abraham settles in a foreign land. Moses leads the Israelites out of Egypt. Joshua leads the Israelites to the Promised Land. David becomes the king of Israel. Solomon constructs a Temple for the Lord. Esther delivers the Jews from a genocide plot. Nehemiah returns to Jerusalem and leads in the rebuilding of its walls. These are but a few of the dozens of people mentioned within the Old Testament that fulfilled a mission from the Lord. It seems each person was given a specific mission or discovered it. Once the mission became clear, the person committed his or her life to fulfilling the mission from the Lord.

NEW TESTAMENT

The Old Testament contains numerous accounts of people who fulfill their mission from the Lord. The New Testament captures the

53. Esther 4:13–14 NIV.
54. Nehemiah 6:15 NIV.

words of Jesus and provides Christians an example of how people can adhere to the biblical mandate. Several passages throughout the Gospels touch on the on the mission of the church and describe a mission for Christians today.

The Gospel of Matthew records the words of Jesus known as the Great Commission. The Great Commission is spoken after Jesus' resurrection and as he prepares to ascend into Heaven. Jesus speaks to his disciples and gives them this challenge: "Therefore go and make disciples of all nations, baptizing them in the name of the Father and of the Son and of the Holy Spirit, and teaching them to obey everything I have commanded you. And surely I am with you always, to the very end of the age."[55] The Great Commission becomes one, if not the primary, mission of the church. The disciples cling to this statement. Today, many churches strive to fulfill this mission. In addition to the book of Acts, the Gospels of Mark and Luke contain similar words to the Great Commission. The Gospel of Mark says, "Go into all the world and preach the gospel to all creation. Whoever believes and is baptized will be saved, but whoever does not believe will be condemned."[56] The Gospel of Luke states, "This is what is written: The Messiah will suffer and rise from the dead on the third day, and repentance for the forgiveness of sins will be preached in his name to all nations, beginning at Jerusalem."[57] The book of Acts records, "But you will receive power when the Holy Spirit comes on you; and you will be my witnesses in Jerusalem, and in all Judea and Samaria, and to the ends of the earth."[58] The Great Commission embodies and fulfills the mission of the church by making disciples.

Some churches may readily reference the Bible or even these passages specifically, but not strive to fulfill them. In a sense, these churches are full of worldly Christians and not world Christians.[59] As Paul Borthwick suggests, we either "focus on ourselves or

55. Matthew 28:19–20 NIV.

56. Mark 16:15–16 NIV.

57. Luke 24:45–47 NIV.

58. Acts 1:8 NIV.

59. Borthwick, *A Mind for Missions*, 13.

on the world around us."[60] Borthwick goes on to explain that "a worldly Christian is one who accepts the basic message of salvation, but whose lifestyle, priorities, and concerns are molded by self-centered preoccupation"[61] and "the worldly Christian's desire for self-fulfillment or personal satisfaction makes his or her perspective very narrow."[62] Borthwick says that "a world Christian breaks the mold of a self-centered way of thinking."[63] If someone claims to be a world Christian, then he or she should strive to fulfill the biblical mission.

HOW CAN A CHURCH WORK TOWARDS FULFILLING THE BIBLICAL MISSION?

A church's mission must be based upon Scripture and the accomplishment thereof. The intent of this book is to revisit the biblical accounts of people who were given a mission from the Lord and Jesus' instruction for the mission of the church and to renew a commitment towards fulfilling the biblical mission for a church, as a case study. Many churches lose sight of the biblical mission of the church and its fulfillment. In their book, *Comeback Churches*, Ed Stetzer and Mike Dodson describe the importance of a renewed belief in Jesus Christ and the Mission of the Church.[64] Here are some elements Stetzer and Dodson provide as to this renewed belief:

> Renewed belief—realizing the daily relevance of Christ and how the mission lines up with that.
>
> Renewed belief—built values around the people's involvement in the mission of the church.
>
> Renewed belief—refocused from the foundation of Scripture upon the mission of the church.

60. Ibid., *A Mind for Missions*, 13.
61. Ibid., *A Mind for Missions*, 13.
62. Ibid., *A Mind for Missions*, 14.
63. Ibid., *A Mind for Missions*, 15.
64. Stetzer and Dodson, *Comeback Churches*, 56.

> Renewed belief in mission—accepted person responsibility for encouraging lost to come to church.
>
> Renewed belief/mission—taking time to refocus on Christ and His mission.
>
> Renewed belief/mission—the church regained a sense of direction based on Christ's mission.
>
> Renewed belief—emphasis placed on our reason for existing.[65]

The renewed belief in Jesus Christ and the Mission of the Church play a vital role in assessing whether a church is aware of and able to determine whether the mission is being fulfilled. Stetzer and Dodson write,

> As a pastor or church leader, you are and will always be— under the headship of Jesus—the key to the church. You are the primary shaper of your church's values, beliefs, strategy, and direction. You set the direction for your people. God calls you to focus on both quality and quantity; not just "how many" but also "how well."[66]

This church is in need of a renewed commitment towards fulfilling the biblical mission of the church. The church, I served, increased to an attendance of over 300 in the mid 1990s but has since then decreased to a plateau attendance of 150 in 2010. A renewed commitment towards fulfilling the biblical mission of the church could help with the change process. A renewed mission establishes the theological framework for implementing a change process. Though some methods may change, the primary mission of the church remains the same. Once this church renews its commitment towards fulfilling the biblical mission of church, then the church can begin to implement and execute its freshly renovated mission. Bob Russell states, "Both the leaders and the congregation need to be constantly reminded of the primary mission of the church."[67] If a leader's task is to help define the mission,

---

65. Stetzer and Dodson, *Comeback Churches*, 57–58.

66. Stetzer and Dodson, *Comeback Churches*, 14.

67. Russell, *When God Builds a Church*, 265.

then the leader must also implement and execute said mission. Just as CEOs define and execute the mission of a business, ministers should work at defining, reiterating, and executing the mission of the church. The next chapter will review concepts as to how to develop and implement a mission.

two

Change

MUCH HAS BEEN WRITTEN about the subject of change. Books on change—whether in a business or in a church—can be found everywhere. This chapter will discuss several resources that have been developed from the business perspective, that were helpful in the change process for this church, as a case study. This chapter will proceed as follows. It will:

1. Review the cultural factor
2. Review the vision framework
3. Review the eight-stage process of creating major change
4. Introduce the development of the change process for a church

THE CULTURAL FACTOR

Edgar Schein says, "Culture matters."[1] He goes on to say,

> Culture is a property of a group. Wherever a group has enough common experience, a culture begins to form. One finds cultures at the level of small teams, families, and workgroups. Cultures also arise at the level of departments, functional groups, and other organizational

1. Schein, *The Corporate Culture Survival Guide*, 3.

units that have a common occupational core and common experience. Cultures are found at every hierarchical level. Culture exists at the level of the whole organization if there is sufficient shared history. It is even found at the level of a whole industry because of the shared occupational backgrounds of the people industrywide. Finally, culture exists at the level of regions and nations because of common language, ethnic background, religion, and shared experience.[2]

Culture is a word not often heard in the context of a church. Culture is spoken of as, for example, the culture of Europe compared to North America, the culture of Los Angeles compared to New York, or the culture of people who live on farms compared to that of people who live near the ocean. Church members do not necessarily consider the different cultures that exist among churches. In business, people tend to see the behavior and hear about a corporate culture. A corporate culture may be something people aspire too and desire to become a part of. Does not everyone want to belong to something meaningful? John Kotter and James Heskett explain the power of corporate culture:

1. Corporate culture can have a significant impact on a firm's long-term economic performance.

2. Corporate culture will probably be an even more important factor in determining the success or failure of firms in the next decade.

3. Corporate cultures that inhibit strong long-term financial performance are not rare; they develop easily, even in firms that are full of reasonable and intelligent people.

4. Although tough to change, corporate cultures can be made more performance enhancing.[3]

Corporate or not, culture becomes ingrained within us. John Kotter and James Heskett write, "The concept of culture was thus

2. Ibid., *The Corporate Culture Survival Guide*, 13–14.
3. Kotter and Heskett, *Corporate Culture and Performance*, 11–12.

coined to represent, in a very broad and holistic sense, the quali-
ties of any specific human group that are passed from one generation to the next."[4] As people belong to an organization, they
are influenced by the culture that exists within. Schein makes the
clear point, "If we want to make organizations more efficient and
effective, then we must understand the role that culture plays in
organizational life."[5] Thom S. Rainer and Chuck Lawless refer to
the following two phrases that are most often heard in churches
regarding change, "We've never done it that way before" and "We
tried it before, but it didn't work."[6] Even though these two statements refer to change, they come from an already established culture that is becoming resistant to change.

Addressing change is a complicated matter in any setting. In
an established setting, the supporting leadership can prepare the
church or other organization for the emergence of a new leader.
Kotter and Heskett state

> The establishment of a strong leadership process, not to
> replace, but to supplement a management process, is an
> absolutely essential part of all of these stories of major
> cultural change. Unlike even the very best manage-
> ment process, leadership has as its primary function the
> production of change. Without leadership, purposeful
> change of any magnitude is almost impossible.[7]

Kotter and Hesket also point out

> This leader must create a perceived need for change even
> if most people believe all is well. He must create and
> communicate effectively a new vision and set of strate-
> gies, and then behave accordingly on a daily basis. He
> must motivate an increasingly large group of people to
> help with this leadership effort. These people must find
> hundreds or thousands of opportunities to influence

4. Ibid., *Corporate Culture and Performance*, 34.

5. Schein, *The Corporate Culture Survival Guide*, 14.

6. Rainer and Lawless, *Eating the Elephant: Leading the Established Church to Growth*, 159.

7. Kotter and Heskett, *Corporate Culture and Performance*, 97–99.

behavior. And the resulting actions on the part of a growing group of people must produce positive results; if they
do not, the whole effect losses credibility.[8]

Again, this shows the need for a competent leadership to
facilitate the change process. John Mawell provides a good statement, "My goal is to develop leaders who become a movement."[9]
A change process includes a foundation for leadership development. As I considered a change process for this church, I had to
take culture into account.

Edgar Schein provides a good resource on identifying the
levels of culture within an organization. The first level is artifacts.[10]
Schein says that "The easiest level to observe when you go into an
organization is that of artifacts: what you see, hear, and feel as you
hang around."[11] Understanding this first level gets you in the door
of an organization. You begin observe all that takes place around,
which inevitably leads to uncovering the second level, espoused
values.[12] Schein states, "To dig deeper means to start asking questions about the things the organization values. Why do they do
what they do?"[13] Asking these kinds of questions helps you understand the actions that are carried out. However, if digging continues, then something else may be found. This leads to the third
level, shared tacit assumptions.[14] The shared tacit assumptions take
into account the history of the organization. As time passes by,
the founding leaders begin to "impose their own beliefs, values,
and assumptions on the people whom they hire."[15] Schein suggests
"Perhaps most important of all, you begin to realize that there is
no right or wrong culture, no better or worse culture, except in

8. Kotter and Heskett, *Corporate Culture and Performance*, 101.

9. Maxwell, *Developing the Leaders Around You*, 3.

10. Schein, *The Corporate Culture Survival Guide*, 15.

11. Ibid., *The Corporate Culture Survival Guide*, 15.

12. Ibid., *The Corporate Culture Survival Guide*, 17.

13. Ibid., *The Corporate Culture Survival Guide*, 17.

14. Ibid., *The Corporate Culture Survival Guide*, 19.

15. Schein, *The Corporate Culture Survival Guide*, 19.

relation to what the organization is trying to do and what the environment in which it is operating allows."[16]

Edgar Schein gives a good, basic definition of culture, "the way we do things around here."[17] In other words, Schein claims, "If you really want to understand the culture, you must have a process involving systematic observation and talking to insiders to help make the tacit assumptions explicit."[18] There are three definite facets to remember: Culture is deep. Culture is broad. Culture is stable.[19] In order to tackle a change process for this church, I could not forget about the cultural factor.

In his book, *Organizational Culture and Leadership*, Edgar Schein describes how culture and leadership complement each other. Schein states

> When we examine culture and leadership closely, we see that they are two sides of the same coin; neither can really be understood by itself. On the one hand, cultural norms define how a given nation or organizations will define leadership—who will get promoted, who will get the attention of followers. On the other hand, it can be argued that the only thing of real importance that leaders do is to create and manage culture; that the unique talent of leaders is their ability to understand and to work with culture; and that it is an ultimate act of leadership to destroy culture when it is viewed as dysfunctional.[20]

Both organizational culture and leadership must understand each other in order to adjust to one another. Throughout his book, Schein provides an extensive analysis of how the two interact. Schein writes, "Learning and change cannot be imposed on people."[21] For a leader to lead in an established culture, learning

16. Ibid., *The Corporate Culture Survival Guide*, 21.

17. Ibid., *The Corporate Culture Survival Guide*, 24.

18. Ibid., *The Corporate Culture Survival Guide*, 25.

19. Ibid., *The Corporate Culture Survival Guide*, 25–26.

20. Schein, *Organizational Culture and Leadership*, 10–11.

21. Ibid., *Organizational Culture and Leadership*, 418.

must occur between the two of them and the world in which the culture exists. Schein concludes,

> In the end, we must give organizational culture its due. Can we recognize—as individual members of organizations and occupations, as managers, as teachers and researchers, and sometimes as leaders—how deeply our own perceptions, thoughts, and feelings are culturally determined? Ultimately, we cannot achieve the cultural humility that is required to live in a turbulent culturally diverse world unless we can see cultural assumptions within ourselves. In the end, cultural understanding and cultural learning starts with self-insight.[22]

In his book, *How the Mighty Fall*, Jim Collins presents research on the stages of decline in organizations. Collins gives an example as to how a culture, when the culture remains unchanged, affects the future of the organization. Collins writes:

> During the Burger era, A&P's arrogant stance that "we will continue to keep things just the way they are and we will continue to be successful because—well, we're A&P!" left it vulnerable to new store formats developed by companies like Kroger. Burger failed to ask the fundamental question, why was A&P successful in the first place? Not the specific practices and strategies that worked in the past, but the fundamental reasons for success. It retained its aging Depression-generation customers but became utterly irrelevant to a new generation. As one industry observer quipped, "Like the undertaker, A&P could have said every time a hearse went by, 'There goes another customer.'"[23]

Offering an explanation to this example, Collins states,

> The point here is not as simple as "they failed because they didn't change." As we'll see in the later stages of decline, companies that change constantly but without any consistent rationale will collapse just as surely as those

---

22. Ibid., *Organizational Culture and Leadership*, 418.
23. Collins, *How the Mighty Fall*, 37.

that change not at all. There's nothing inherently wrong with adhering to specific practices and strategies (indeed, we see tremendous consistency over time in great companies), but only if you comprehend the underlying why behind those practices, and thereby see when to keep them and when to change them.[24]

In essence, the culture of an organization affects whether it rises or falls. If the culture does not change, it may fall. If the culture changes, it may fall. There needs to be an appropriate culture to implement change in a way that it may raise.

Once I began serving as the senior minister, I began realizing a culture already existed. This church had been in existence for over 50 years, therefore a culture had already been established. Even though I had several conversations with the previous senior minister and church leaders before my arrival, I had not considered the culture of the church as deeply as I should have. I would have described the culture of this church as that of a traditional church.

In their book, *Eating the Elephant: Leading the Established Church to Growth*, Thom S. Rainer and Chuck Lawless describe the difference between a nontraditional and traditional church. While traditional churches are not necessarily ineffective, there are obstacles that may arise when the senior minister addresses change in light of the culture of the church. Of course, every church and culture is different. The culture of a business, or church, may determine its receptiveness to change.

During my tenure as senior minister of this church, I had observed that currently the culture of the church is traditional and more resistant to change. Furthermore, I was convinced this culture may affect the change process.

24. Ibid., *How the Mighty Fall*, 38.

VISION FRAMEWORK

"A high-profile, charismatic style is absolutely not required to suc-
cessfully shape a visionary company."[25] Although some may think
that a charismatic visionary leader is needed, that is not always the
case. What is needed is a leader that looks at building and developing something beyond him—or her. Jim Collins writes, "Level 5
leaders want to see the company even more successful in the next
generation, comfortable with the idea that most people won't even
know that the roots of that success trace back to their efforts."[26]
One could compare Jim Collins' statement regarding businesses
with the Great Commission spoken by Jesus in that both would
see the organization and church to be successful in future generations. For churches, this would suggest that they should work
towards fulfilling the biblical mission, a mission that is based upon
Scripture and executing Jesus' vision of the church. Therefore, a
church can fulfill the biblical mission of the church by discerning
its existence within the culture in which a local church is established. By considering the vision framework, a church may be able
to articulate its mission and vision within its cultural context.

In his book, *Strategic Thinking: Pure & Simple*, Michael Robert describes the power of vision. Robert writes, "First and fore-
most, it captures the organization's "future intent." In other words,
it paints a "picture" of what the company intends to become, not
what it is today."[27] Robert claims that a vision "bonds, inspires, is
an anchor, is a potent competitive tool" and "must be clear, compelling, distinctive, and consistent."[28] However, to implement steps
toward that vision, a strategy is needed. Robert points out that
a "strategy determines what you want to become as a company
and operations determines how you get there."[29] In order for an

25. Collins and Poras, *Built to Last*, 32.

26. Collins, *Good to Great*, 26.

27. Robert, *Strategic Thinking: Pure & Simple*, 49.

28. Ibid., *Strategic Thinking: Pure & Simple,* 49–51.

29. Ibid., *Strategic Thinking: Pure & Simple,* 51.

organization to strive towards fulfilling its vision, it must have a strategy to get there.

In their book, *Built to Last*, Jim Collins and Jerry Porras present a tool for developing a vision framework. Collins points out that "in truly great companies, change is a constant, but not the only constant. They understand the difference between what should never change and what should be open for change, between what is truly sacred and what is not."[30] The vision framework serves as that constant. Collins writes, "the fundamental distinguishing characteristic of the most enduring and successful corporations is that they preserve a cherished core ideology while simultaneously stimulating progress and change in everything that is not part of their core ideology."[31] Collins goes on to state, "Put another way, they distinguish their timeless core values and enduring core process (which should never change) from their operating practices and business strategies (which should be changing constantly in response to a changing world).[32] The vision framework is a tool designed to clarify the mission and values and establish goals to achieve.

The vision framework consists of the core ideology and an envisioned future. Collins defines the core ideology and envisioned future this way: "it defines "what we stand for and why we exist" that does not change (the core ideology) and sets forth "what we aspire to become, to achieve, to create" that will require significant change and progress to attain (the envisioned future).[33] The core ideology component within the vision framework remains constant, while the envisioned future is adaptable. The two work together. This is worth examining closer.

The first part of the vision framework is core ideology. Collins describes core ideology as "the enduring character of an organization—its self-identity that remains consistent through time and transcends product/market life cycles, technological

30. Collins, *Built to Last*, 220.
31. Ibid., *Built to Last*, 220.
32. Ibid., *Built to Last*, 220.
33. Ibid., *Built to Last*, 221.

breakthroughs, management fads, and individual leaders."[34] Core ideology becomes a foundation for which the organization is built. For churches, the Great Commission slides right into that role. It is up to each congregation to phrase the Great Commission, or biblical mission of the church, in a way that is indigenous to its cultural context, so that the church is distinct in its location and culture.

Within the core ideology, core values need to be identified. Collins says, "Core values are the organization's essential and enduring tenets—a small set of timeless guiding principles that require no external justification; they have intrinsic value and importance to those inside the organization."[35] Core values are unique to the church or other organization. Collins notes that "these values must stand the test of time."[36] Collins presents a simple exercise that can be used in identifying about five values. To paraphrase, imagine you are part of a community establishing a colony on Mars. Your task is to articulate a set of values which will stand the test of time and that are unique to your community's culture.[37] What would your community be known for? By wrestling with similar questions, you and your group should be able to narrow down a set of values that would be unique for your organization, or church.

In addition to the core values, a core purpose needs to be identified. Collins claims that the core purpose is "the organization's fundamental reason for being."[38] A core purpose, or mission, needs to be stated. As discussed in chapter one, the biblical mission of the church can take the place of the core purpose. Again, the core purpose can be written or verbalized in a way that is unique to each congregation.

The second part of the vision framework is the envisioned future. Collins describes the envisioned future this way: "On the one hand, it conveys a sense of concreteness—something vivid and

34. Ibid., *Built to Last*, 221.
35. Ibid., *Built to Last*, 222.
36. Ibid., *Built to Last*, 222.
37. Ibid., *Built to Last*, 223–224.
38. Ibid., *Built to Last,* 224.

real; you can see it, touch it, feel it. On the other hand, it portrays a time yet unrealized—a dream, hope, or aspiration."[39] The envisioned future becomes a picture like-goal which the organization may become. For churches, this may mean discovering and discerning what the church is capable of within its cultural context.

Within the envisioned future, BHAGs, or "Big Hairy Audacious Goal," should be developed. These BHAGs should be set at a "vision-level;" in other words, it should take 10 to 30 years to achieve.[40] The BHAGs can be attained, but will take time, hard work, and the involvement of everyone. The BHAGs motivate everyone to unite and focus on that objective.

In addition to BHAGs, a vivid description should be utilized. Collins states that a vivid description is "a vibrant, engaging, and specific description of what it will be like to achieve the BHAG."[41] From another perspective, a vivid description is like "picture-painting."[42] The vivid description of the church is articulated in the Bible[43], but can also serve a specific purpose within its community. For instance, the vivid description of a local church may be to become a place that meets the needs of those who are hungry, therefore a soup kitchen or food pantry is created. Another church may partner with a non-profit organization to serve domestic violence victims.

In this case study, it was an opportune time to analyze the vision of this church. If there was not a vision already in place, then the leadership, consisting of elders, deacons, and ministry staff, could utilize the vision framework in the change process.

39. Ibid., *Built to Last*, 232.
40. Ibid., *Built to Last*, 232.
41. Ibid., *Built to Last*, 233.
42. Ibid., *Built to Last*, 233.
43. Acts 2:32–42 NIV.

EIGHT-STAGE PROCESS FOR CREATING MAJOR CHANGE

In his book, *You Can't Order Change: Lessons from Jim Mcnerney's Turnaround at Boeing,* Peter S. Cohan writes about "the leadership style and practices of Jim McNerney."[44] Cohan describes Jim Mc-Nerny as "a leader who gets results by motivating others."[45] Cohan's observations highlight many techniques in dealing with corporate cultural change. Cohan points out McNerney's successive leadership as CEO in two different companies, 3M and Boeing. In both, McNerney increased sales change, profits, and growth. According to Peter Cohan, McNerny addresses the necessary changes that are needed to take place in order to turn the company around. This process is referred to as "The McNerny Way."[46] Here is a breakdown of "The McNerny Way:"

> Place Leadership Development at the Top of Your Priority List.
>
> Pursue Strategies That Spark Organic Growth
>
> Tighten Operations to Reduce Costs and Increase Productivity
>
> Establish More Harmonious Relationships with Communities[47]

Cohan offers additional insights into McNerney's leadership style. Many of these insights could be beneficial to anyone undergoing change at any level in any organization, profit or non-profit, business or church. Therefore in order to move forward with a change process, one should utilize a change approach.

No one ever said change would be easy. In all types of organizations, profit, non-profit, public, private, businesses, or churches, change can be difficult on all fronts and all levels. Either people will react positively or negatively to change. Whether it is a minor

44. Cohan, *You Can't Order Change,* 1.
45. Ibid., *You Can't Order Change,* 7.
46. Ibid., *You Can't Order Change,* 10.
47. Ibid., *You Can't Order Change,* 11–14.

change, such as parking in a different spot, or a major change, such as unveiling a new strategy, leading a change process is tough. In his book, *Leading Change*, John P. Kotter provides eight reasons as to why organizations may fail:

> Error #1. Allowing Too Much Complacency
>
> Error #2. Failing To Create A Sufficiently Powerful Guiding Coalition
>
> Error #3. Underestimating the Power of Vision
>
> Error #4. Undercommunicating the Vision By a Factor of 10 (Or 100 Or Even 1,000)
>
> Error #5. Permitting Obstacles to Block The New Vision
>
> Error #6. Failing to Create Short-term Wins
>
> Error #7. Declaring Victory Too Soon
>
> Error #8. Neglecting To Anchor Changes Firmly In the Corporate Culture[48]

When businesses hire well-known executives or churches extend an invitation to a younger, energetic pastor, both leaders will face challenges. Businesses, as well as churches, should define the roles and responsibilities of its leaders to address change. Kotter states, "Leadership defines what the future should look like, aligns people with that vision, and inspires them to make it happen despite the obstacles."[49] If this is clearly understood by those in leadership positions, then perhaps there can be a proactive approach to leading change. If not, then, as Kotter puts it, "bureaucracy and an inward focus take over."[50] Kotter claims, "The key lies in understanding why organizations resist needed change, what exactly is the multistage process that can overcome destructive inertia, and, most of all, how the leadership that is required to drive that process in a socially healthy way means more than good

48. Kotter, *Leading Change* , 16.
49. Ibid., *Leading Change*, 25.
50. Ibid., *Leading Change*, 27.

management."[51] Kotter writes, "The methods used in successful transformations are all based on one fundamental insight: that major change will not happen easily for a long list of reason."[52] In other words, change is not easy. Therefore, John Kotter presents a valid case in order to face major change. As Kotter puts it, one of the driving forces behind change is "leadership, leadership, and still more leadership." As mentioned in chapter one, a major function of a leader is to define the mission of the business or church, and a primary function of a leader is to regularly and consistently remind the business or church of its mission. If a leader helps define the mission, then a leader must also be willing and able to lead a business or church through a change process to return to its original mission.

In his book, Kotter presents an eight-stage process for leading change. The first stage is establishing a sense of urgency because "establishing a sense of urgency is crucial to gaining needed cooperation."[53] This first stage addresses complacency. Kotter goes on to say, "never underestimate the magnitude of the forces that reinforce complacency and that help maintain the status quo."[54] In order to wrestle with complacency, a leader must raise the urgency level. In other words, what will we do if this or that happens? If we continue to do and perform the same way, where will that lead us? If we are focusing on target A and we desire target B, what will we need to do? What needs to change? By considering the outcome of remaining the same, perhaps a sense of urgency can be established. In the book, *The Heart of Change*, John Kotter and Dan Cohen offer tips on what works and what does not work for increasing urgency.

The second stage is creating a guiding coalition. This involves developing a team that will be honest and proactive in leading change. Kotter claims, "Change often starts with just two or three

51. Ibid., *Leading Change*, 16.
52. Ibid., *Leading Change*, 20.
53. Ibid., *Leading Change*, 36.
54. Ibid., *Leading Change*, 42.

people."[55] Depending upon the organization, time can be a major player. It takes time to build trust and a team who can help lead change. Unfortunately, the current condition of the organization can sometimes hinder progress. If the present condition is moving from bad to worse, then time makes it that much harder to lead change. Kotter suggests that "the combination of trust and a common goal shared by people with the right characteristics can make for a powerful team."[56] Kotter and Cohen offer suggestions on how to build the guiding team.

The third stage is developing a vision and strategy. Kotter writes "Vision refers to a picture of the future with some implicit or explicit commentary on why people should strive to create that future."[57] A vision shows some activity or organization as it will be in the future; it is a set of possibilities realistic and easy to communicate.[58] A clear vision is a strong driving force to becoming what the organization is capable of being. A vision that is attached to the mission can help maintain focus. A vision builds on the mission. Both are needed for the change process. Kotter and Cohen provide suggestions to get the vision right.

The fourth stage is communicating the change vision. Kotter states,

> A great vision can serve a useful purpose even if it is understand by just a few key people. But the real power of a vision is unleashed only when most of those involved in an enterprise or activity have a common understanding of its goals and direction. That shared sense of desirable future can help motivate and coordinate the kinds of actions that create transformation."[59]

Leaders can be creative in communicating the vision. Kotter presents key elements in the effective communication of a vision:

55. Kotter, *Leading Change*, 59.
56. Ibid., *Leading Change*, 65.
57. Ibid., *Leading Change*, 68.
58. Ibid., *Leading Change*, 71–72.
59. Ibid., *Leading Change*, 85.

I affirm that leadership is key. It is vital that leadership continues to clarify the mission and vision of the organization to keep it on track. If leadership is not revisiting the mission, then the organization may become sidetracked and lose focus. Kotter urges that "without sufficient leadership, change stalls, and excelling in a rapidly changing world becomes problematic."[65] Kotter and Cohen also refer to this concept as, "Don't let up."

The eighth and final stage is anchoring new approaches in the culture. Kotter states,

> "Culture is powerful for three primary reasons: 1. Because individuals are selected and indoctrinated so well. 2. Because the culture exerts itself through the actions of hundreds or thousands of people. 3. Because all of this happens without much conscious intent and thus is difficult to challenge or even discuss."[66]

As discussed earlier, culture becomes and continues to be an important component of the change process. As Kotter so eloquently puts it, "The biggest impediment to creating change in a group is culture."[67] To wrap it all up, Kotter states, "It is because such change is so difficult to bring about that the transformation process has eight stages instead of two or three, that it often takes so much time, and that it requires so much leadership from so many people."[68]

I agree with Kotter's conclusion about this eight-stage process for leading change:

> In the twentieth century, the development of business professionals in the classroom and on the job focused on management—that is, people were taught how to plan, budget, organize, staff, control, and problem solve. Only in the last decade or so has much thought gone into developing leaders—people who can create and communicate visions and strategies. Because management deals

65. Kotter, *Leading Change*, 144.
66. Ibid., *Leading Change*, 150–151.
67. Ibid., *Leading Change*, 155.
68. Ibid., *Leading Change*, 158.

mostly with the status quo and leadership deals mostly with change, in the next century we will have to become much more skilled at creating leaders. Without enough leaders, the vision, communication, and empowerment that are at the heart of transformation will simply not happen well enough or fast enough to satisfy our needs and expectations.[69]

By examining the cultural factor, the vision framework, and eight-stage process for creating major change, I was able to begin developing a change process for this church.

DEVELOPING A CHANGE PROCESS

Each of the previously reviewed areas—the cultural factor, the vision framework, and the eight stage process for creating major change—affects the development and implementation of a change process. The cultural factor, vision framework, and the eight stage process for creating major change stem from the original mission. Each has a relationship with the other. A clear mission must be established in order to develop a change process. In the case study, a clear mission had to be firmly established to develop a change process for this church. The next chapter will explain the development and implementation of the change process for this church, utilizing the concepts of the cultural factor, vision framework and eight-stage process for leading change.

69. Kotter, *Leading Change*, 165.

II

New Wine into Old Wineskins

three

Case Study

It HAS BEEN SAID that "Theory without implementation accomplishes little." The previous two chapters have examined the challenge and opportunity for a church to address change, by understanding the biblical mission of the church, and reviewing resources that address the change process. Each chapter has dealt with theories in addressing the change process, specifically for the church I served.

In their book, *Comeback Churches*, Ed Stetzer and Mike Dodson write, "If it [change] was easy, everybody would be doing it!"[1] This is a response to the question, how do you change it (church)? Stetzer and Dodson simple state, "Change is hard."[2] I affirm the words of Stetzer and Dodson. Since this church faced changes, I undertook this challenge as a leader participant-observer to explain my journey and provide conclusions regarding the development and implementation of a change process for this church.

The aim of this case study is not only to look at theories, but to implement and assess the execution of those theories for this church. This chapter will explain how these theories, when implemented, helped the change process for this church. This chapter will present:

1. Stetzer and Dodson, *Comeback Churches*, 23.
2. Ibid., *Comeback Churches*, 23.

- Four workshops used to lead a change process
- A timeline and resources used to communicate the implementation of the change process

FOUR WORKSHOPS TO LEAD A CHANGE PROCESS

Imagine interviewing for a senior minister or pastor position for an established church. What types of questions would you ask about the church, its leadership, its strategies, its policies, or its organizational infrastructure? Where would you turn for advice or input for considering its present state? How would you know if a church is, or has been, fulfilling its biblical mission? How would you determine if the leadership of the church is ready for change? Change in leadership is not always easy, either for the new, or emerging, leader or for the church. Change has not been easy.

Once I began serving as the senior minister, I started contemplating those questions I could and should have asked during the interview process. I asked; what tools are available in addressing the change process? How can the church and I be prepared for this change? Therefore, I decided this was an opportunity to realign with the biblical mission of the church, to assess its mission, its values, its strategy, and its vision. In order to focus on the mission, clarify the values, align the strategy, and cast a vision for this church, I developed the following four workshops for the leadership to pray about, discuss, reflect, and implement. By conducting these workshops, I lead a change process for this church through which the leaders, members, attendees and future members could articulate the purpose of this church.

GETTING STARTED

I FIRST MET WITH the elders and ministry staff and instructed them that I wanted to revisit the biblical mission of the church, so that as we moved forward we could all be in agreement. The previous senior minister had served for over forty years. A new senior minister meant change was taking place. I wanted to affirm the previous senior minister's ministry and affirm what would not change—the beliefs and practices of the Restoration Movement— even though the leadership had changed. I had begun serving as the senior minister about a month after the previous senior minister retired. I wanted the leadership to understand a philosophy of ministry: how we would approach why we do what we do, and how we would do ministry.

When we met, I presented a schedule (Appendix A) where the leadership would meet four times for two hours each session. Each session would allow us to pray together, dialogue and develop a change process for this church. Each session would address one major question towards developing a change process this church. At the beginning of the first session, I stated the expectations for this change process: what I hoped this team would accomplish (Appendix B).[3] These expectations would help as we moved forward. Once the expectations were stated, we prayed about the process and dove into the first session.

FOCUS ON THE MISSION

To get started, I distributed a session handout (Appendix C) and we began with the first big question: Why change? We discussed why we needed to change aspects of how this church conducted ministry. This may not have been the best question to start with since I had only been the senior minister for about six months. Asking this question implied that there was something wrong or that something needed to be fixed. Over the course of his first six months as senior minister, I had been presented with this question head on. It seemed to me that this church wanted to embrace change, but did not really understand what that meant for the church. From my perspective, change meant a new preaching and teaching style, new ideas, and new expectations from the

3. These expectations were developed from Aubrey Malphurs' *Advanced Strategic Planning*. I rephrased his "covenant of commitment" to provide some guidelines for the leadership of this church.

congregation. While it appeared to some that only a few changes would be satisfactory, some deeper changes needed to be explored. As discussed in a previous chapter, change would involve a closer look at the cultural factor, since the previous senior minister's tenure was over forty years.

I dove into the first workshop by discussing the question, Why change? The premise for asking this question originated from Ed Stetzer and Mike Dodson's book, *Comeback Churches*. This book analyzed churches that were considered stagnant or dying and how those churches were able to implement changes that ignited growth. The book explores and presents several findings that could be used in helping a church turn around. Stetzer and Dodson claim, "Based upon the results of the comeback surveys, it is apparent that churches desiring a comeback will need to make changes in order to start growing again."[4] Stetzer and Dodson state "the average person in a church believes that the church exists to meet his or her needs and the needs of the family."[5] If this is the prevailing attitude and perception, then it only makes sense to ask the question "why change?"

Based on his reading of *Comeback Churches*, I thought this question would be appropriate at the time. Besides, Stetzer and Dodson say, "Churches wanting change must discuss, discuss, discuss."[6] If there were any changes that needed to be identified and addressed, then at least the leadership would have an opportunity to discuss those changes together. Here are some of the thoughts and comments in response to the question "why change:"

- For growth
- Emphasis on young people
- Stop changing, start dying
- No major change in last 10-15 years because of opposition
- Aging congregation

4. Stetzer and Dodson, *Comeback Churches*, 27.
5. Ibid., *Comeback Churches*, 29–30.
6. Ibid., *Comeback Churches*, 30.

- Little involvement
- Low expectations
- Limited space for classrooms, parking, and land

Stating these reasons gave me some insight into the current condition of this church with regard to demographics, physical resources, and previous change efforts. Although the discussion could not cover every single reason as to why change at this church was necessary, it did give the elders and the ministerial staff a starting point to continue the discussion. Since this workshop, there have been opportunities to continue the discussion.

After raising the question, "Why change?" I thought it would be worthwhile to focus on the biblical mission of the church. I then led a study on biblical examples of people on a mission and God's mission for the church. The leadership read and studied the Bible. It appeared to me, at the time, that everyone was unanimous with the biblical mission of the church. At that point, I instructed everyone to summarize, or paraphrase, the biblical mission of the church in a single phrase short enough to fit on a t-shirt. This phrase would become a rallying cry, a renewed mission that could keep us in check; one that could be evaluated qualitatively and quantitatively.

By the end of the first session, the leadership began discussing values that this church should be known for and that could be used to describe what is important to this church. Each participant created a list, and then shared them. Here are some of those initial values:

- Community
- Service
- Excellence
- Prayer
- Family-oriented
- Welcoming

The next session would continue the discussion with regard to those values.

CLARIFY THE VALUES

At the end of the first session, the elders and ministerial staff of this church had begun brainstorming values that this church should be known for and that could be used to describe what is important to this church. Chapter two reviewed, in greater detail, the importance of values. Upon arriving at this church, I did not find any clear values stated in written form. Therefore, I thought it would be vital to clarify the values in order to proceed with the change process.

In the second session, I distributed a session handout (Appendix D) and asked the question, "Who do we want to reach?" The reason I asked this question was to see if the elders would describe the current demographic of this church, as well as its hoped-for future demographic. We discussed this question. Below are several issues and questions that were raised during this discussion:

- The immediate community surrounding the location consisted of an aging residential neighborhood where many of the residents were retired.

- There is a challenge of connected churches (other churches in the community) whereby friends and family are involved and those friends and family gravitate towards each other (thus members being involved in two different churches).

- A number of young families had moved out of the area in search of jobs.

- It seems there are a number of transient people—people residing in the community for less than two years.

- How can this church serve the community around us?

- How can this church connect men and families?

- How can this church involve members and non-members?
- How can this church focus on younger families?
- How do the building and grounds of this church affect a younger demographic?
- Does an aging building affect curbside appeal for families?
- Does current parking and spacing reflect an appealing family-friendly atmosphere?

This discussion opened a floodgate of new questions. However, I believed that these questions spurred a healthy conversation about the current condition of this church.

Once we had spent time discussing and considering the original question of "Who do we want to reach?" I urged everyone to consider the strengths and weaknesses, its opportunities, and potential threats to the church. This appeared to me to be a new way of looking at the ministry and effectiveness. It was interesting to me to realize that the question, "Who do we want to reach?" carried over to a new topic. The building and grounds were mentioned as both strengths and weaknesses. The building and grounds were an extension of the church, and affected who this church wanted to reach. Basically nothing was said about opportunities and threats, which indicated to me that strategic planning had not been discussed extensively in the past. As a leader participant-observer, I was provided further insight into the current state and condition of this church.

At that point I thought we should spend the rest of the time clarifying the values this church. I believed a set of values would help them determine who we wanted to reach, as well as identify some areas where this church could improve in order to execute those values. These values would come from a collaborative effort of this team, to help us set the course in which we wanted to head. In his book, *Advanced Strategic Planning*, Aubrey Malphurs describes it this way:

> Core values explain who you are—your identity. They are the very building blocks (DNA) of your ministry and

explain why you do what you do. They form the foundation on which the mission and vision build, and along
with them form the church's core ideology. In naviga-
tional terminology, they function like the GPS (Global
Positioning System) that tells the navigator where the
ship is.[7]

A set of core values would prove valuable in any future discussions. I wanted the leadership to articulate, in written form, the
values of this church. So in the rest of session two, we identified
five values which we thought would describe what this church
should be known for, and used to describe what is important to
this church. Each person created a list of values, then the group
shared the responses with each other. Here is an extensive list of
those values that were mentioned:

- community
- family-oriented
- welcoming
- accepting
- friendly
- evangelistic
- biblical
- relevant
- involved
- dedicated
- believing
- giving
- independent
- mission
- personal
- needs met

7. Malphurs, *Advanced Strategic Planning*, 96.

- fellowship
- satisfied
- caring
- focused
- commitment
- unity

Of this list, I combined those that were similar and identified five values that we all agreed on: community, family-oriented, biblical, involved, and mission. These five values had already been woven into the fabric and culture of this church. By identifying the values, we would be able to utilize them in future discussions.

ALIGN THE STRATEGY

At the conclusion of the second session, the elders and ministerial staff had accomplished what I had hoped to achieve. We were focusing on the mission and had arrived at a consensus statement that we could use to communicate the mission. We were clarifying the values by reaching a consensus of values that we believed represented the past and future of this church. Through these two sessions, we had been "discussing, discussing, and discussing"[8] ways in which this church could change. I believed that once we had laid this foundation, we could proceed with aligning the strategy to accomplish our mission and live our values.

At the beginning of the third session, I reviewed what we had already accomplished by distributing a session handout (Appendix E). I reviewed this handout and what we had concluded. Here is a summary:

- Focus on the Mission:
  - » Why does this church exist?
  - » Pointing People to Jesus

---

8. Stetzer and Dodson, *Comeback Churches*, 30.

- Clarify the Values:
  - » What is important to this church?
  - » Community, Family-Oriented, Biblically Relevant, Involved, Mission-minded

I thought these sessions would be good groundwork for the elders and ministerial staff to help us understand each another, and also to understand how I viewed my role as senior minister. These sessions would be foundational in communicating my view of ministry, and what I perceived as my role and responsibilities as a leader and senior minister.

At this point, I outlined a way in which we could align the strategy with the mission and values that we had discovered. To begin this discussion, which lasted about an hour, I asked this question: How will this church live its mission? I then presented an approach using the letters, G (Grow), P (Participate), and S (Share).

I developed this strategy utilizing Thom Rainer and Eric Geiger's book, *Simple Church*. Rainer and Geiger define a simple church as ". . . a congregation designed around a straight-forward and strategic process that moves people through the stages of spiritual growth."[9] Through research, Rainer and Geiger came to this expanded definition of a simple church:

> A simple church is designed around a straightforward and strategic process that moves people through the states of spiritual growth. The leadership and the church are clear about the process (clarity) and are committed to executing it. The process flows logically (movement) and is implemented in each area of the church (alignment). The church abandons everything that is not in the process (focus).[10]

Rainer and Geiger provide greater explanation to these four key words. They define clarity as "the ability of the process to be

9. Thom Rainer and Eric Geiger, *Simple Church* (Nashville: B & H Publishers, 2006), 60.

10. Ibid., *Simple Church*, 67–68.

communicated and understood by the people;"[11] movement as "the sequential steps in the process that cause people to move to greater areas of commitment;"[12] alignment as "the arrangement of all ministries and staff around the same simple process;"[13] and focus as "the commitment to abandon everything that falls outside of the simple ministry process."[14] Throughout their book, they make a compelling argument using the simple strategy as method of change. Therefore, I incorporated the simple church methodology into his presentation on how to align the strategy with the mission and values of this church.

At this church, the (G) Grow component would enable a person to grow in his or her relationship with God by attending a weekly worship service. The (P) Participate component would be when a person could participate with other believers through Sunday School, a Bible study, or Equip U. The (S) Share component would be when people could share their faith and resources through inviting others to church, sharing their personal testimony, and giving of their time, talents and treasures. This strategy would utilize many of the ministries and programs which were already in place, giving them deeper purpose.

Once I presented GPS as an answer, to how will this church live its mission, there was little discussion. Everyone seemed to understand and be in agreement with one another. This strategy was simple to understand and to communicate. At that point, we discussed and brainstormed goals within the GPS strategy. However in the midst of the brainstorming, the conversation began shifting towards what other churches were doing in their area, comparing themselves with those churches, and what had been done in the past and proven effective at one point in time. At the end of this session, I was hopeful everything was understood and communicated well, but then found myself leaving confused as to what had just happened. We still had the fourth session to complete.

11. Ibid., *Simple Church*, 70.
12. Ibid., *Simple Church*, 72.
13. Ibid., *Simple Church*, 74.
14. Ibid., *Simple Church*, 76.

CAST A VISION

The fourth and final session addressed the question, what will this church look like in five years? The previous three sessions were to focus on the mission, clarify values, and align the strategy. Now, the task which lay before the elders and ministers was to develop some long-range goals, or BHAGs: Big Hairy Audacious Goals.[15] As I saw it, the change process was coming to fruition.

At the beginning of the fourth session, I distributed the session handout (Appendix F). I reviewed what we had accomplished up to this point. The elders and ministerial staff had been able to answer three main questions:

- Why does this church exist?
  - » Pointing People to Jesus (Matthew 28:19-20; Mark 16:15; Luke 24:46-48; Acts 1:8)
- What is important to this church?
  - » We value Biblical relevance. (Acts 2:42)
  - » We value community. (Acts 2:44)
  - » We value mission-minded. (Acts 2:45)
  - » We value involvement. (Acts 2:46)
  - » We value families. (Acts 2:46-47)
- How will this church live its mission?
  - » GROW: Sunday Worship
  - » PARTICIPATE: Adult Groups
  - » SHARE: Serve

After reviewing the change process, we spent the remaining time discussing and describing what we hoped this church would look like in five years. A number of goals were discussed. Here are several of those goals mentioned:

15. Jim Collins and Jerry I. Porras, *Built to Last* (New York: HarperCollins, 1997), 89.

- Enhance music ministry
- Add contemporary service
- Increase member involvement
- Implement CORE courses
- Every member to lead at least one person to Christ
- Yearly short-term mission trip
- Updated parking
- Updated facilities/capital improvements
- Connection Café
- Involvement Drive
- Church "with" or "of" small groups

After listing these goals, the group proceeded to discuss and prioritize them. We discussed and identified the goals that challenged us, as well as what was reasonable to achieve. We didn't want to set any goals that were too high, because we didn't want to feel defeated before we had even begun. Once we chose those goals, we were able to assign the goals to correspond to the strategy that was built on the values and the mission. It seemed that the change process was being realized.

Here were the goals as corresponding to the strategy:

GROW: Goals—Enhance music ministry & Add contemporary worship service

PARTICIPATE: Goals—60%+ involvement & Implement CORE courses

SHARE: Goals—Every member to lead at least one person to Christ & Yearly short-term mission trip

At the conclusion of the fourth session, the leadership seemed satisfied with our results. We had accomplished what we had set out to do. We were able to visual components to cast a vision for the future of this church. With the development of the change process behind us, we then had to proceed with communication and execution.

IMPLEMENTATION OF THE CHANGE PROCESS

In order to implement the change process for this church, I needed to communicate this change process to the congregation. The elders and ministerial staff began these workshops in May 2010 and concluded in July 2010. At that point, it was time to begin integrating the change process into communication pieces—such as the weekly bulletin, newsletter, and website—to be unveiled to the congregation on October 3, 2010. The development and execution of the change process gave me, who was the senior minister, an opportunity to cast a vision and to lead by communicating the change process to the congregation.

When October 3, 2010 arrived, we were ready to unveil the mission. We integrated the mission: Pointing People to Jesus! into communication pieces. We purchased a banner with the mission printed on it, and put it on permanent display.

During the October 3, 2010 worship service, an elder shared his story of people who were involved in Pointing People to Jesus! A video was shown of an interview with someone who told the history of how this church had been Pointing People to Jesus! I then preached a series entitled, Pointing People to Jesus! over the course of five weeks. This series was designed to communicate the change process to the people. Instead of trying to explain in one hour, I taught a series. The first sermon was Pointing People to Jesus!, which explained the mission. The second sermon, GROW, addressed the first step in the strategy. The third sermon, PARTICIPATE, tackled the second step in the strategy. The fourth sermon, SHARE, dealt with the third step in the strategy. The fifth sermon, VALUES, described the hoped-for values. The sermon series allowed me to communicate the change process to the people. At the conclusion of the October 3, 2010 worship service, we conducted a Celebration Sunday Meal, which had been coordinated weeks earlier, to celebrate what God had done in the past and what

God could do in the future. The final chapter is my assessment of the change process for this church since its development and implementation.

four

Considerations

ASSESSMENT

THERE ARE SEVERAL THINGS I had learned since the development and implementation of a change process for this church. As mentioned earlier, this church has been in existence for over 55 years. Of those 55 years, there have only been four senior ministers, including myself. To note, there have been individuals who have served as Associate Minister, Youth Director, or Christian Education Director during the existence this church.

As a leader participant-observer in the change process for this church, there are seven lessons that I have learned from the change process. This chapter will offer my thoughts 1) as the leader participant-observer, 2) as a new senior minister in an established church, and 3) as a lifelong learner. Each lesson will consider each of these perspectives within its explanation. In the conclusion, I will introduce a simple tool that a new minister, young or old, could use as the candidate considers a call to an established church. This tool could be used to discern the infrastructure of the established church.

SEVEN LESSONS LEARNED FROM THE CHANGE PROCESS

LESSON #1 LENGTH OF TENURE

First, the length of tenure of the senior minister of a church can greatly impact defining the mission and casting a vision. Since this church had only had four senior ministers in her existence, there has been a limited turnover in senior ministerial staff. The length of tenure for the first and second senior ministers were short compared to the third senior minister. The third senior minister's length of tenure was forty-two years of the fifty-five years of this church's existence. It would seem that there was a healthy relationship between this church and senior minister for his ministry to last as long as it did.

With over forty years of ministry, that senior minister shaped the culture of this church. Whether they realize it or not, the length of tenure of the this senior minister greatly impacted his parishioners' experience. Many of his strengths and abilities were unveiled over the course of his ministry. Many people built strong and lasting relationships with him, and grew accustomed to his style of ministry. The length of his tenure gave him the opportunity to interact with multiple generations within a family. For instance, he not only married a couple, but was there when the couple gave birth, was present when that child graduated high school, and even available when he or she began a family. He was present for the many milestones in his parishioner's lives, whether spiritual, social, or physical.

With a new senior minister many people were faced with uncertainties. The people were now in a situation which they had not experienced in many of the parishioners' lifetimes. This was a real challenge for me, the new senior minister. Now there was a new person, younger with a different education and diverse experiences. I had not grown up in the area, and therefore was not as familiar with the history and culture. I was aware of a few things that I was exposed too through the interviewing process, but a weekend and a few hours in phone conversations did not prepare me for what I was entering. The people had their expectations of what a new senior minister would bring, as well as, I would expect from them as the new senior minister. As a new senior pastor, to begin a change process within the first six months of my ministry was not the best approach. Many people had stated they wanted and expected change, but were they really prepared for what it might entail. Was I prepared for what it might entail?

LESSON #2 THE CULTURE

Second, the culture of the people greatly impacts the mission and vision of the church. Again, since my predecessor's length of tenure was over forty years, a certain kind of culture existed. I greatly underestimated the impact of the culture of this church. I saw my pastorate as an opportunity to change culture, and for the most part, I think this church wanted a cultural change. However, I do not think this church realized the difficulty in changing its culture. For instance, early on, I was faced with the question, how do we reach a younger demographic? During my first year, I made several observations. Older members were asking that question. Younger members and visitors were replying that the dress code, the traditional music, the same format, traditional special music, the building, and the colors of the upholstery were not appealing and reminded them of the time period the building was constructed—the 1970s. Also, this church did not have an updated website. A younger audience uses the internet on a consistent basis, but this church had a limited online presence. Some wanted to divert funds to advertising in the local newspaper, whereas I was leading the people to utilize a website where we could publish more information. I observed that, part of the culture of this church was to use the local newspapers instead of the internet.

The culture goes beyond the artifacts. It includes the behaviors and norms of the people. There seems to be a common language among the people. As an outsider coming in, even though I am the new senior minister, it was hard to break into the cultural norm which has existed for so long. I did not know all the people or their stories. In some ways, I was expected to know many of these people and their stories prior to any new situations. When a conflict arises, I did not have all the prior experiences, which leaves me scrambling to gather all of the past information in order to address a problem. I did not know all of the people and their experiences early in my tenure, which became a disadvantage to me. As discussed in chapter two, the cultural factor became a major component in addressing change. Any new senior minister beginning in an established church, especially where there has been little senior minister turnover, faces the cultural challenge head on. Without any knowledge or prior experiences with the established church, the senior minister is at a disadvantage in the church.

LESSON #3 LEADERSHIP DEVELOPMENT

Third, a lack of a clear leadership development process affects the future leaders. Upon beginning my tenure I observed and participated in various leadership meetings. As I recall, there was no leadership development taking place. I spoke with several lay leaders and volunteers and they stated they had not been trained or equipped properly to do their jobs. One lay leader, who was a deacon, did not know what a deacon was or what he was supposed to do.

The practice this church was to nominate and vote on lay-leaders yearly, without the candidates undergoing any training process. It seemed as though the purpose of an election was to fill the voids with warm bodies. This left many questioning what it is that they are supposed to do within the roles that they possess. There is no clear direction and people are left scrambling and asking what their responsibilities are.

A lack of leadership development can hinder the growth of any organization, whether a church or business. If a lay-leader could not clearly and readily explain his or her roles and responsibilities, then how can this church continue to forge ahead in the future? This is a challenge to overcome and an opportunity to pursue. I believe any candidate would have to tread extremely

New Wine into Old Wineskins

cautious in a similar situation. Even at monthly leadership meetings, there was no formal agenda except maintenance requests and other such issues within the church, because the present leaders had not been equipped. Since the leaders had not been equipped, how would they be expected to proceed in addressing any of the deep concerns that are brought forward?

LESSON #4 DEMOGRAPHIC

Fourth, a changing demographic in the surrounding community must affect how the mission and vision of this is executed. During the senior minister interviewing process, I was able to visit the community and drive around the area. I conducted online research on cost-of-living, population, local government, economic statistics, newspapers, and the history of the town. Even though I read a lot about the area, I still had not experienced much of it myself. I did not have any history or experience with the parishioners or the surrounding communities.

During the interview process, the lay leaders and the congregation indicated that they were an aging/older congregation and were interested in striving to reach a younger demographic. Being in my late twenties at the time of my interviews, I felt as though I could identify with the younger demographic. However, as I participated in the interview process, I realized many customs and practices could readily be considered "old-fashioned" or "traditional." I saw this as both a challenge and an opportunity to be undertaken by the church. The building and grounds were well-maintained, however, the interior reflected the era in which it was constructed, or last renovated. This, too, would prove challenging in reaching a younger demographic.

As I became familiar with the town, I learned that several industries had closed and laid off hundreds of people, so unemployment had increased. Because of this, many young families were planning to relocate in search of employment. One advantage in the area was the number of higher educational institutions that existed. A disadvantage was that the students would move after graduation. How will this church reach and retain a younger demographic in an aging and increasing retirement community? A number of young families had moved or begun attending other churches because of the aging congregation, its practices, and its customs. The composition of aging/retired people in the community and this church add to the challenges of targeting a younger demographic. With so many factors, it was difficult to work towards this goal.

LESSON #5 A LACK OF STRATEGIC PLANNING

A lack of strategic planning affects the potential opportunities of this church. Throughout the interview process and upon my arrival, there were no strategic plans, either long-range or short-term. There was no particular vision being cast, whether ideologically or physically. Although the exterior of the building and grounds was maintained and in good working order the interior possessed many flaws. For instance, carpets were worn and outdated, paint colors had fainted, and there were leaks in the building. Even though these examples related to building and grounds, there were no plans of any sort to address capital improvements. Signs were posted stating "no trespassing, no skate boarding, no bicycling, and no ball playing," yet there was a basketball hoop located on the edge of the parking lot. This sends a mixed message. Without any strategic planning, the expectations of hopes of reaching a younger demographic would be challenging because the interior care of the building could reflect the care of people. Would a young couple feel comfortable leaving their child in an unsafe, unclean environment?

Strategic planning goes beyond the building and grounds to take into consideration how ministry should be accomplished and why. Strategic planning incorporates the mission of the church, its values, and its vision. If these are not understood or communicated, then ministry exists without any clear purpose. It becomes difficult to lead, cast vision, motivate, and inspire people to do what they are capable of. I believe this church has struggled in the past and even in the recent years prior to my arrival because there was no strategic plan. People have left because they were not inspired to help the church pursue its potential.

Upon my arrival, I wanted to lead a change process in hopes of rediscovering the biblical mission for the church. I believe that by discovering this mission, a new vision could be cast with a new senior minister.

LESSON #6 INFRASTRUCTURE

Sixth, a lack of a strong infrastructure, or support system, affects those who were already serving. There was an informal line of communication and no clearly defined organizational chart among lay leaders and staff. This created obstacles for everyone. No one knew what others were doing or planning to do, and this proved challenging for the paid staff. This was also true of the lay leaders because volunteers did not know exactly where to turn to for support and guidance. Some groups took it upon themselves to do whatever they wanted within the building, such as purchasing equipment or using funds without staff or lay leader approval. A lack of infrastructure keeps people or leaders from being accountable. Without some form of accountability, many problems could develop.

Infrastructure is like a frame in house. The house cannot stand without the proper support. It seems that this church had functioned for many years without a strong infrastructure, thus the church had its share of problems between paid staff and lay leaders. Churches, like all organizations, need an infrastructure to stand. This infrastructure can be adapted to fit its needs.

If a change process had been developed before I began serving, then there should be an infrastructure to support its execution. After we concluded the four workshops and moved to implementation, I began to see that a stronger support system between ministerial staff and lay leaders was needed for the church to reach its maximum potential. I asked about the infrastructure or an organizational chart of communication at this church, but nobody seemed to know or wanted to define it at the time. I felt this would be important for the present and future of this church.

LESSON #7 A LACK OF POLICIES & PROCEDURES

Seventh, a lack of a clear outline of policies and procedures affects how ministry gets accomplished. The lack of policies and procedures indicates the lack of an infrastructure. I believe this frustrates many people. Without policies and procedures, miscommunication ensues. For instance, someone with a good idea would want everyone else to support his or her idea. A clearer process of policies and procedure could help the person and the idea receive greater support from everyone. This would also filter out unnecessary ideas. Within my first ninety days, I had to decide whether to continue every ministry, activity, and event that had been done prior to my arrival. I decided not to because that would create a schizophrenic ministry. A schizophrenic ministry pursues every idea and continues every activity while adding more activities. This church was not able to focus on doing a few things well; instead it appeared to be doing many mediocre things. Policies and procedures could filter the undue strain on the church. For instance, policies and procedures would help with communicating to the congregation and allocating resources to the appropriate ministry for maximum impact. If a new ministry did not align with the strategy, then clear policies and procedures could help the ministry do so or be dropped.

Instead of doing ministry as it had always been done, I wanted to lead a change process, so that the people could focus and do ministries well. I felt a change process would be a good starting point in course correcting. I believe ministry happened without purpose or even understanding why a particular activity or event was executed. By rediscovering what this church was about, we could make a greater impact, besides I thought this was part of striving to be a leader. A change process would help define a purpose for ministry. Two of the tasks which a leader cannot delegate are leadership development and changing the culture. I firmly believed that a change process would be a way to both develop leaders and change culture by determining where she should go and how she could get there.

The change process has taught me to rely upon God. These seven lessons were uncovered through the change process for this church. Even if I had learned these lessons earlier in my ministry, it would not have meant that everything would be perfect. The people and the culture play such an important role in how these lessons are applied. These seven lessons may be applied differently in another context because of the culture and the leaders. As someone once put it, "Everything rises and falls on leadership" and what we need more of is "leadership, leadership, leadership." Not only that, but we need leaders willing to change.

As the elders and ministerial staff underwent this project and began to focus on the mission, clarify the values, align the strategy, and cast a vision, these seven lessons were uncovered. The project became more than a task to complete in an established church. It became an organizational, sociological and leadership experience which has taught me that a change process is more than a theory and more of a practice over the course of time. Any change involves time whether a brief moment or an extended period. Although the goal of this book was to lead this church through a change process, it became a leadership lesson for me. A change process would prove not only to be beneficial to this local church, but also a refining experience for me to become a servant leader.

The goal of this project was to reflect upon this church and to develop a change process for her. Through the four workshops a dialogue was begun to rediscover the mission of the this church within her context. There are numerous and differing churches, some with denominational ties and others that are non-denominational, some sharing a similar mission to this church and a specific role within the community. A church is strongly influenced by the culture of the external community and that of the internal community. The makeup of the surrounding communities can determine how a church will define its mission and execute its strategy. As a new senior minister of this church, I believe this was a good time to revisit what the mission and strategy are for this church. A new senior minister can bring change for an already established church, especially for this church. By conducting the four workshops, a tool has been created to help future ministers and servant leaders discern God's call upon their respective churches. This tool could help future leaders determine whether an established church has considered its mission and its strategy. If the mission and strategies have been considered, the tool helps the leader understand why the particular church exists and how well the church executes its strategy. If not, it helps the leader develop a dialogue, or a starting point, to make sure that the church is meeting a need within the community.

A TOOL FOR A NEW MINISTER IN AN ESTABLISHED CHURCH

Any new senior minister of any age, beginning a ministry in an established church could ask the following four questions to determine if the leadership of an established church has considered her direction:

1. Why does (name of church) exist?
2. What is important to (name of church)?
3. What will (name of church) look like in 5 years?
4. How will (name of church) live its mission?

These four questions were derived from the four workshops. I wish I had considered and explored these questions in greater depth in my interview process. I believe these questions could have helped me gauge the ability of the church to handle the change process.

The first question determines the biblical mission of the established church. Has the established church clearly defined and articulated its mission? If so, then what is it? Is it communicated in an indigenous way? By stating the mission in the church's own words, the church takes on the mission as part of their identity, rather than trying to be like someone else. If it is not articulated, then would you consider discovering it for your church? By doing this at this church, the mission has become a rallying cry. It is stated often in speech and publication. We can measure how well we are doing against the phrase. The mission for this church is Pointing People to Jesus! We have had members share how and who have pointed them to Jesus. These stories show the interconnectedness and how we are fulfilling the biblical mission of the church.

The second question determines the values of the established church. Has the established church considered its values? If so, then what are the values? If the values are not stated, then would you search for them? A clear set of values can communicate what is important to your church and what your church wants to be known for. The values will help identify who and how ministry is executed. By identifying the values at this church, the leadership is able to design ministries that incorporate those values. For instance, one of the values at this church is family, so this church planned events for the whole intergenerational family such as WinterBlitz. WinterBlitz was basically a game night where children played games with senior adults. Seeing a male teenager interact with a retired grandmother was heartwarming. Another example is coordinating meals that allow people to interact. This incorporates the value of community.

The third question determines the vision of the established church. Has the established church communicated a vision, or picture, of its future, extending to at least five years from now? If so, then what is it? Are there clearly defined goals for the church, its ministries, and its staff? If not, then perhaps you can discover a vision for your church. A five year vision helps the church strive towards a goal. A lot can be accomplished in the span of five years. For instance, this church has identified enhancing the music ministry as a five year goal. This church intends to move from traditional songs to utilizing more contemporary songs. This church has also begun integrating this through the Worship Choir. The Worship Choir has also been able to incorporate the value of involvement by recruiting additional people. This church would also like to encourage sixty percent or more member involvement, which is another five year goal. So not only has a value been addressed, but also steps toward the goal have been taken.

The fourth question determines the strategy of the established church. Has the established church prayerfully developed a plan for the church to live its mission? If so, then how? If not, then what are the best ways for the church to accomplish it mission? A strategy will help assimilate people into your church. At this church, GPS, (G stands for Grow, P stands for Participate, and S stands for Share) is the strategy, whereby people can grow in their relationship with God by attending weekly worship, participate with other believers by attending a Sunday School class, and share their faith and resources by being involved and inviting others. The strategy also directs people to take their next step in their faith development, a step which requires greater commitments, yet is simple enough to do each week. Many churches expect everyone to be involved with everything, which could lend to burnout and being overwhelmed. A simple strategy also helps people fulfill the mission.

If these questions are answered completely, then they prove useful for the incoming senior minister. If these questions are not answered completely, then they may help the incoming senior minister to develop a change process and lead the church to where it has not been before with God's guidance. This simple practical tool may help the incoming senior minister to assess the state of the established church.

Appendix A

May 18, 2010—Workshop I: Focus on the Mission

June 19, 2010—Workshop II: Clarify the Values

July 22, 2010—Workshop III: Align the Strategy

August 3, 2010—Workshop IV: Cast a Vision

September 3, 2010—Promotions (bulletin, newsletter, website, etc.)

October 3, 2010—Unveil the change process to this church via Sermon Series, Communication Pieces, Celebration Meal

Appendix B

TEAM EXPECTATIONS

Team Expectations:
1. To pray for the church, team, and the process
2. To be a positive team player who will support the process
3. To support team consensus decisions even when I don't agree
4. To be at the meetings as much as possible
5. To keep matters confidential
6. To commit to the process

Appendix C

SESSSION ONE: Why Change?

Focus on the Mission

What was the mission for each of the following?

- Exodus 3:10-(Moses)
- 2 Samuel 5:2-(Daniel)
- Nehemiah 2:17-(Nehemiah)

What is God's mission for the church?

- Matthew 28:19-20
- Mark 16:15
- Luke 24:46-48
- Acts 1:8

Describe the mission in a single phrase, short enough to fit on a t-shirt.

Clarify the Value

Write down 7 values that this church should be known for and is used to describe what is important to this church.

Appendix D

Who do we want to reach?

- Strengths:
- Weaknesses:
- Opportunities:
- Threats:

Focus on the Mission

&

Clarify the Values

Appendix E

SESSION THREE

Focus on the Mission

Why does this church exist?

P_____ P_____ to J_____!

Matthew 28:19-20; Mark 16:15; Luke 24:46-48; Acts 1:8

Clarify the Values:

What is important to this church?

- Community
- Family-oriented
- Biblically relevant
- Involved
- Mission-minded

Align the Strategy

How will this church live its mission?

G_____.

P_____.

S_____.

Cast a Vision:

What will this church look like in 5 years?

GROW Goals:
PARTICIPATE Goals:
SHARE Goals:

Appendix F

SESSION FOUR

Focus on the Mission:

Why does this church exist?
Pointing People to Jesus!
Matthew 28:19-20; Mark 16:15; Luke 24:46-48; Acts 1:8

Clarify the Values:

What is important to this church?
- We value Biblical relevance. (Acts 2:42)
- We value community. (Acts 2:44)
- We value mission-minded. (Acts 2:45)
- We value involvement. (Acts 2:46)
- We value families. (Acts 2:46-47)

Align the Strategy:

How will this church live its mission?
GROW
- Primary: Sunday Worship
- Secondary: CORE Seminar

PARTICIPATE
- Primary: Adults Groups
- Secondary: Adult Ministry Events

SHARE
- Primary: Serve
- Secondary: Monthly Share Projects

Cast a Vision:

What will this church look like in 5 years?

GROW Goals:
- Enchance music ministry
- Add contemporary worship service

PARTICIPATE Goals:
- 60%+ involvement
- Implement CORE courses

SHARE Goals:
- Every member to lead at least on person to Christ
- Yearly short-term mission trip

Bibliography

Barna, George. *Leaders on Leadership*. Ventura: Regal, 1997.

Bennis, Warren. *On Becoming a Leader*. New York: Basic, 2009.

Blackaby, Henry T. and Richard Blackaby. *Spiritual Leadership*. Nashville: Broadmand & Holman Publishers, 2001.

Borthwick, Paul. *A Mind for Missions*. Colorado Springs: NavPress, 1987.

"Christian CEO's on Leadership." *www.preachingunleashed.com*. Smart Ministry Archives. June 2010.

Cohan, Peter S. *You Can't Order Change*. New York: Penguin Group, 2008.

Collins, Jim. *Good to Great*. New York: HarperCollins, 2001.

———. *How the Mighty Fall*. New York: HarperCollins, 2009.

Collins, Jim and Jerry I. Porras. *Built to Last*. New York: HarperCollins, 2004.

Gardner, John W. *On Leadership*. New York: Free , 1990.

Harper, Tom R. *Leading from the Lion's Den*. Nashville: B & H Publishing Group, 2010.

Hellweg, Eric. "The Eight-Word Mission Statement." *Harvard Business Review*. 22 October 2010.

Kotter, John P. *Leading Change*. Boston: Harvard Business School Press, 1996.

Kotter, John P. and Dan S. Cohen. *The Heart of Change*. Boston: Harvard Business School Press, 2002.

Kotter, John P. and James L. Heskett. *Corporate Culture and Performance*. New York: Free, 1992.

Malphurs, Aubrey. *Advanced Strategic Planning*. 2nd Edition. Grand Rapids: Bakerbooks, 2005.

Maxwell, John C. *Developing the Leaders Around You*. Nashville: Thomas Nelson, 1995.

Rainer, Thom and Chuck Lawless. *Eating the Elephant: Leading the Established Church to Growth*. U.S.: Pinnacle Publishers, 2003.

Rainer, Thom and Eric Geiger. *Simple Church*. Nashville: B & H Publishers, 2006.

Robert, Michael. *Strategic Thinking: Pure & Simple*. Norwalk: PPS, 2004.

Rusaw, Rick and Eric Swanson. *The Externally Focused Church*. Loveland: Group,2004.

Bibliography

Russell, Bob. *When God Builds a Church.* West Monroe: Howard Publishing Co., 2000.

Sander, J. Osawld. *Spiritual Leadership.* Chicago: Moody, 1967.

Schein, Edgar H. *The Corporate Culture Survival Guide.* San Francisco: Jossey-Bass, 1999.

————. *Organizational Culture and Leadership.* 3rd Edition. San Francisco: Jossey-Bass, 2004.

Senge, Peter. "The Leader's New Work: Building Learning Organizations." *Sloan Management Review.* Fall 1990.

Stanley, Andy and Bill Willits. *Creating Community.* Sisters, Oregon: Multnomah Publishers, 2004.

Stetzer, Ed and Mike Dodson. *Comeback Churches.* Nashville: B & H Publishing Group, 2007.

Taylor, Mark. "Help for the Time You Hire a New Minister." *Christian Standard.* 10 October 2010.

Thrall, Bill, Bruce McNicol, and Ken McElrath. *The Ascent of a Leader: How Ordinary Relationships Develop Extraordinary Character and influence.* New York: John Wiley and Sons, 1999.

Warren, Rick. *The Purpose Driven Church.* Grand Rapids: Zondervan Publishing House, 1995.

www.ingramcontent.com/pod-product-compliance
Lightning Source LLC
Chambersburg PA
CBHW071105090426
42737CB00013B/2492